THE EVOLUTION OF TELEWORK IN THE FEDERAL GOVERNMENT

Wendell Joice, PhD
Office of Governmentwide Policy
US General Services Administration

February 2000

CONTENTS

PART ONE: GENERAL EVOLUTION

CONCLUSION: TODAY

THE EVOLUTION OF TELEWORK IN THE FEDERAL GOVERNMENT

PART ONE: GENERAL EVOLUTION

INTRODUCTION

This paper documents the evolution of the Telework movement in the Federal government. This movement, which has spanned the last quarter century, is still unfolding and has yet to reach its zenith.

AN EVOLUTION OF WORKPLACE CHANGE

The history of Federal telework reflects the evolution of one of the most significant and progressive changes in work conditions for Federal employees. Beginning during the last decade of the 20th century, the Federal telework movement reflected that period's interest in workforce impact on family, environment, and general quality of life. It was also one of the most important barometers of the transition from industrial age to information age human resources and workplace management. It is a classic study of the struggle for change in a 20th century bureaucracy. Interestingly enough, it also shows how the efforts of a relatively few resulted in a potential impact on the worklives of 1.8 million Federal workers.

THE SEMANTICS OF 'TELEWORK': TELEWORK = TELECOMMUTING = FLEXIPLACE

Since the inception of telework, there has been a continuing controversy over terminology. Terms such as telework, telecommuting, and Flexiplace have been widely used and confused. There has been a lack of consensus as to (1) what each of these terms means and (2) the difference between their definitions. For ease of communication, we will sidestep this issue as follows: for the purposes of discussion in this paper, we will treat the terms telework, telecommuting, and Flexiplace as synonyms that refer to the following:

A work arrangement

> A work arrangement in which an employee regularly works at
> an alternate worksite such as the employee's home, a
> telecommuting center (Telecenter), or other alternate
> worksite. A telecommuting *alternate worksite* is any
> facility, in which the employee works, which saves that
> employee a more lengthy commute (distance-wise and/or
> time-wise) to a main worksite.

> A *main worksite* is any facility where the employee would
> normally perform work if there were no alternate worksite.

> To be considered telecommuting, the work done must be in
> paid status. Thus, for example, working at home extra hours
> for which the employee is not paid is *not* telecommuting.

OVERVIEW

The evolution of Federal telework can be viewed as occurring in
several stages. An initial spurt of activity occurred in the late
70's and early 80's and appeared to fade out by the mid 80's.
This activity consisted of small scale pilots and experiments
conducted separately by individual agencies. A second stage,
featuring the first governmentwide Flexiplace pilot, began in
1989. This pilot focused on work-at-home arrangements. A third
stage introduced Federal telecommuting centers (telecenters) and
began in 1993. The activity levels of stages two and three began
to diminish somewhat and, in 1996, stage four, the National
Telecommuting Initiative (NTI), was implemented. This
governmentwide initiative contained ambitious goals (such as
60,000 Federal teleworkers by September of 1998). NTI activity
waned considerably by mid-1998 and plans were undertaken for a
reenergized NTI. The re-energized NTI, when implemented, will
represent a fifth stage. As of this writing, the latter activity
is still being defined and planned.

To provide an accurate context for this history, the reader
should note the following:

- This paper focuses on the development of formal Federal
telework programs which are characterized by formal policies,
procedures, and regular telework work schedules. This discussion
does not focus on the continuing use of informal work-at-home
practices utilized by many agencies [In a study conducted in 1989

(Cowley & Joice, 1989), it was found that a substantial number of Federal agencies were already utilizing informal, as-needed telework arrangements that were established typically on a case-by-case (individual employee) basis].

- Preceding and paralleling the history of formal Federal Flexiplace is telework activity related to employees with disabilities. Federal agencies such as DOD, Labor, GSA, and HHS all played active roles in this arena. The history of telework and physically challenged employees is a saga of its own, and while it will be discussed briefly below, the interested reader should see other sources (such as Hesse (1995) or Joice (1991)) for more detail.

THE EARLY DAYS

JACK NILLES: ORIGINATOR OF TELECOMMUTING

One of the earliest governmentwide policies relating to Federal telework was in 1957 when the Comptroller General approved payment of salaries, on a case-by-case basis, to Federal employees for work done at home (see historical reference in GAO, 1992). The earliest effort to generate a Federal telework program, however, appears to have occurred in the early 60's when Jack Nilles, commonly considered to be the father of telework, began teleworking from Los Angeles to Washington, DC while working as a consulting rocket scientist to the US Air Force Space Program. Inspired by this experience, Nilles coined both the words "telecommuting" and "teleworking" in 1973. He began promoting the value and importance of the concept and thus gave birth to the telework movement.

Nilles (Nilles, 1999) suggests some irony in the fact that although he coined 'telecommuting/telework' in conjunction with research that was largely funded by the Federal government (National Science Foundation), he was unable to generate Federal interest in telework. This early lack of Federal interest enabled the state government of California to earn the distinction of being the first major public sector entity to adopt telework:

> "... after completing the NSF project in 1974, I was unsuccessful in inducing any other federal agency to test telework or support further research on it (it was no one's "mission"). So I ended up talking the state of California into it a decade later in order to have a platform for making the impact results public." (Nilles, 1999)

FRANK SCHIFF: ORIGINATOR OF FLEXIPLACE

The first person to generate Federal experimentation with telework was Frank Schiff. At the time, Schiff was Vice President and Chief Economist for the Committee for Economic Development. In 1979, Schiff published an article in the Washington Post in which he challenged the Federal Government to look at management practices, union rules, and Federal laws and regulations in an effort to facilitate working at home as a means of improving productivity, saving costs, and saving energy (this was at the height of the energy crisis during that period). During that same time, Schiff coined the term "Flexiplace" to "encompass not only work-at-home but also such other flexible location arrangements as satellite work centers. Flexiplace would be regarded as a natural complement to the already existing Federal 'Flexitime' program. Moreover, in contrast to such terms as 'telecommuting', it stressed increased flexibility in the location of work, whether or not this is based on the use of telecommunications equipment." (Schiff, 1993)

Schiff's coining of the term 'Flexiplace' is all the more noteworthy since, eventually, the first governmentwide telework program would be called Flexiplace for the reasons provided above by Schiff. In fact, as of this writing (more than a decade after the initial implementation of governmentwide Flexiplace), many Federal agencies still refer to their telework programs as 'Flexiplace'.

Schiff's efforts led to a study conducted by the US Office of Personnel Management, "Flexiplace: An Emerging Issue in Federal Employment":

> The OPM paper first described the basic rationale for Flexiplace. It cited a 1973 legal opinion by the Civil Service Commission (OPM) which stated that there were no laws which required Federal employees to perform their work at a particular site. The paper then described various existing or planned experiments with Flexiplace in the private sector as well as the Federal Government....The paper did not make any formal recommendations but was clearly favorable to the Flexiplace concept. Unfortunately, the report came out just five days before the 1980 Presidential election and the entire effort was apparently discontinued when the new Administration took over (Schiff, 1993)

According to Schiff, the OPM report detailed a group of small-scale Federal agency efforts: General Services Administration (individual teleworker), Department of Labor (disabled employee), Railroad Retirement Board (satellite work station), NASA (neighborhood office center), and IRS (revenue agents).

OTHER EARLY FEDERAL WORK-AT-HOME ACTIVITY

Two additional early work-at-home experiments were conducted at the National Institutes of Health and the Department of the Army. The Army experiment, conducted at an Army facility in St. Louis, was an 18 month activity implemented in 1980 to overcome work scheduling difficulties. Despite the fact that the program performed successfully (project manager evaluations), an army audit team concluded that the potential benefits were exceeded by the risks of fraud and abuse. As a result, the project was discontinued. (Schiff, 1993)

> Interestingly enough, I have learned that the Army auditors privately admitted they would have approved the project if it had been sponsored by a private firm. They were simply afraid that with all the talk about fraud and abuse, the Army would expose itself to too much criticism if it allowed people to work at home!

> This experience helps to illustrate why ... Flexiplace programs petered out by the early 1980's. The emphasis of the new Administration was on reductions in force and on eliminating waste, fraud and abuse, and this was not conducive to experimentation with Flexiplace. The lesson is that if Flexiplace is to prosper, it needs the active, visible, and sustained support of the people at the top.(Schiff, 1993)

Despite the fact that the trend of single agency experimentation with Flexiplace was fading out by the end of the 80's, there was still some noteworthy activity. In July of 1989, the Environmental Protection Agency (EPA) implemented a six month Flexiplace pilot study at its Research Triangle Park facility in North Carolina. This small pilot began with 11 participants and was eventually extended. While the final report indicated some significant problems, it was generally positive about the feasibility of Flexiplace arrangements. The following year, the

Department of the Air Force implemented a six-month pilot at several of its facilities.

AN EARLY EXAMPLE OF TELEWORK AS EMERGENCY RESPONSE

October, 17 1989, brought the Government an early experience with telework as an emergency response strategy. At 5:04 pm that day, the Loma Prieta earthquake severely damaged the EPA Region 9 office building in San Francisco, displacing nearly 800 employees. EPA responded by establishing an auxiliary command post for 80 employees and work-at-home arrangements for the remaining 700+ workers. By March, 1990, 60% of the displaced employees were back in traditional (temporary) workstations while the other 40% continued in Flexiplace awaiting the opening of a new office building. EPA conducted several studies of this experience, learned quite a bit about the feasibility and utility of Flexiplace as both a general workplace strategy as well as an emergency response strategy, and continues to use Flexiplace. Following are a sample of findings from one of the EPA studies (National Analysts, 1991):

- One long-term effect from the earthquake experience about which there was a great deal of agreement was that there should be some kind of work-at-home policy.

- Most of the interviewed managers and staff favored continuation of the work-at-home program.

- While noting that this unplanned and suddenly-implemented program was not an indication of the performance of a normally implemented program, the study pointed out problems such as getting supplies and services, inadequate home environments/space, and psychological discomforts for some of the workers.

THE OLDEST FLEXIPLACE PROGRAM

Finally, one agency, the National Credit Union Administration (NCUA), probably has the distinction of having the longest running formal Federal telework program. As early as 1934 when the NCUA was the Federal Credit Union Bureau, credit union examiners conducted their examinations at credit union sites and then completed their reports at home. Neither the NCUA nor its predecessor provided office space for credit union examiners. Without much fanfare, the NCUA implemented a work-at-home program for its auditors that is still operating successfully.

THE GOVERNMENTWIDE FLEXIPLACE YEARS

THE MOTIVATION FOR A GOVERNMENTWIDE FLEXIPLACE PROGRAM

In the late 1980's, there was an intense public focus on an anticipated drop in the quality of the workforce entering the 21st century. This focus, which was especially pronounced among the nation's employers, was in part instigated by dire predictions stemming from a Department of Labor report entitled Work Force 2000 (Hudson, 1988). In response, the US Office of Personnel Management (OPM) published a similar report, Civil Service 2000 (Hudson, 1988), which focused on the Federal employment picture. The following captures the essence of this report:

> "The Federal government faces a slowly emerging crisis of competence. For years, many Federal agencies have been able to hire and retain highly-educated, highly-skilled workforces, even though their wages, incentives and working conditions have not been fully competitive with those offered by private employers. But as labor markets become tighter during the early 1990's, hiring qualified workers will become much more difficult. Unless steps are taken now to address the problem, the average qualifications and competence of many segments of the Federal workforce will deteriorate, perhaps so much as to impair the ability of some agencies to function." (Hudson, 1988, p. 29)

This report and increasing concerns resulted in a Federal push for solutions, especially non-salary incentives to enhance Federal recruiting and retention. One such solution, adopted by OPM, was to conduct a small telework pilot based on research and recommendations on home-based employment (Joice, 1989).

A FASCINATING OCCURRENCE

Before OPM could implement its Flexiplace pilot, a fascinating chain of events took place. A reporter scouring a Federal management report (over 200 pages) (OMB, 1990), discovered and became interested in the following one-liner:

> Federal agencies will also begin pilot testing of employees "working at home."(p. 2-32)

This was the only mention of Flexiplace in the entire report. Pursuing this, the reporter discovered and publicized the aforementioned OPM plans. This publicity drew the attention of the President's Council on Management Improvement (an umbrella group of agency associate directors for administration)(PCMI). After some brief discussions between OPM and the PCMI, an interagency PCMI task force led by OPM and GSA was established to plan and implement the first governmentwide Flexiplace project. Thus, the development of this landmark initiative was facilitated by the aforementioned work of an enterprising reporter from the Federal Times newspaper.

THE PCMI GOVERNMENTWIDE FLEXIPLACE PROJECT

In January of 1990, the PCMI approved and implemented its task force plans and guidelines for a governmentwide Flexiplace pilot. The "Guidelines for Pilot Flexible Workplace Arrangements" (PCMI, 1990) was a comprehensive document that eventually served as the primary boilerplate for Federal agency Flexiplace policies as well as for numerous private sector and state/local telework programs. The basic tenets of these guidelines are still being used today.

FLEXIPLACE IMPLEMENTATION - EARLY RESULTS

Flexiplace implementation plans called for one-year pilot tests to be conducted by participating agencies and evaluated by OPM. The tests, which were to be conducted over an 18 month period ending in October 1991, were expected to cover between 1500 to 2000 participants.

The First Year:

Getting Flexiplace off the ground was a challenge. While 30 agencies initially expressed interest in participating, only six agencies actually implemented programs during the first year. In fact, six months after the official implementation, Flexiplace had no participants and some very worried project managers. By September of 1990, however, the first three agencies,

- Animal and Plant Health Inspection Service (Department of Agriculture),
- Equal Employment Opportunity Commission, and
- Department of Interior, had implemented Flexiplace programs. Other agencies followed and by the end of 1990 there were about 200 total participants.

THE FIRST FEDERAL PERSONNEL MANUAL LETTER ON FLEXIPLACE

In March of 1991, OPM issued the first Federal Personnel Manual letter (OPM, 1991) on Flexiplace. This letter, FPM letter 368-1, encouraged agencies to participate in the pilot project and provided, as an attachment, the initial Flexiplace FAQ's.

THE FINAL REPORT ON THE WORK-AT-HOME COMPONENT OF FLEXIPLACE

In January, 1993, OPM published a final report (OPM, 1993) on the work-at-home component of Flexiplace. At that time, approximately 700 Federal employees from 13 agencies were participating in Flexiplace. The report was positive and recommended that the PCMI endorse Flexiplace for use by Federal agencies. In October, 1993, OPM sent a memorandum to Federal personnel directors confirming agency authority to utilize Flexiplace arrangements, encouraging agencies to use Flexiplace, and providing guidance on its use.

INITIAL WHITE HOUSE AND CONGRESSIONAL SUPPORT

Beginning as early as 1990 and continuing throughout the evolution of Federal telework, the program has enjoyed bi-partisan political support from both the executive and legislative branches of government. In 1990, President Bush endorsed telecommuting on several occasions: "Telecommuting means saving energy, improving air quality and quality of life. Not a bad deal" (Wheeler, 1990). During the same year, the US Department of Transportation (DOT) included telecommuting in its Statement of National Transportation Policy which cited the rapid advancement of telecommunications technology as providing for a "wide variety of options" in the way people perform their work. Moreover, the Policy stated that such technology would allow the decentralization of business operations and thus permit more employees to work at home.

THE TELEPHONE BILL

The year 1990 also marked the beginning of a long and significant track record of Federal telework support and involvement by Rep. Frank Wolf (R, Va). Working collaboratively at that time with Senator Ted Stevens (R, Alaska), Rep. Wolf introduced a bill that would allow Federal agencies to pay for extra telephone lines, related equipment, and fees needed in the homes of Federal telecommuters. This bill, which was signed into law by President Bush in November of 1990, removed one of the early barriers to Federal telecommuting. Initially, this legislation was in the form of a temporary exemption that was re-issued by Congress on an annual basis. In 1996, however, the legislation was made permanent.

INITIAL CONGRESSIONAL REQUIREMENT TO ASSESS TELEWORK IMPACT

In September, Congress passed an amendment (Wheeler, 1991) to the DOT appropriations bill that required DOT and the Department of Energy to evaluate "the economic, social, and public interest impact of the practice of telecommuting." Senator Conrad Burns (R, Montana), the sponsor of the amendment presented the amendment to President Bush, who eventually signed the package into law.

NATIONAL PERFORMANCE REVIEW

In 1993, the Clinton administration began a series of actions designed to encourage the growth of Federal telework. That year, the National Performance Review (NPR) recommended that GSA and

OPM develop a legislative proposal to enable Flexiplace and telecommuting arrangements for more Federal employees. It further recommended that DOT create and evaluate telecommuting programs (NPR, 1993).

GSA/DOT LEADERSHIP ERA

In 1994, there was a slight changing of the guard for governmentwide telework leadership. GSA and DOT began working together to lead the movement. Both agencies had been charged with telework development responsibilities and realized that collaborative leadership was in their best interests. OPM continued to play an important and supportive role. During this period, telework drivers such as 'family friendly workplaces' and the 'national information infrastructure' (information highway, etc.) arrived on the scene. The chronology for this is as follows.

THE CLINTON FAMILY FRIENDLY WORKPLACE MEMO #1

In a July 1994 memorandum to all Federal agencies, President Clinton adopted the National Performance Review's recommendation that a more family-friendly workplace be created by expanding opportunities for Federal workers to participate in flexible work arrangements.
> "in order to recruit and retain a Federal work force that will provide the highest quality of service to the American people, the executive branch must implement flexible work arrangements to create a "family-friendly" workplace."

The memo further directed that
- The head of each agency (1) establish a program to encourage and support the expansion of flexible family-friendly work arrangements, including telecommuting and satellite work locations and (2) identify barriers and recommendations for addressing such barriers to the President's Management Council.

- OPM and GSA (1) work with agencies to support and expand implementation of flexible work arrangements, (2) promptly review and revise regulations that are barriers to such work arrangements, and (3) develop legislative proposals, as needed, to achieve the goals laid out in the memo.

- The President's Management Council (PMC) and the Office of Management and Budget provide any necessary guidance.

In response to the above memo, OPM and GSA collaborated on a Telework Workshop for Federal managers and OPM (OPM, 1995) published a report on Federal government progress in helping employees meet their work and family responsibilities.

THE NATIONAL INFORMATION INFRASTRUCTURE

In 1994, the Clinton Administration established a priority partnership with the private sector to develop an advanced information infrastructure for the US: the National Information Infrastructure (NII) (NIST, 1994). An interagency and public/private task force, led by the National Institute of Standards and Technology (US Department of Commerce) was established to shape the vision of the NII. Participating on that task force and focusing on how the NII could impact both work and personal life, GSA (Master and Joice, 1994) put together a white paper detailing how telecommuting can be an NII application that can improve the quality of life. Along with seven other papers on NII applications, the telecommuting paper was published with quite a bit of fanfare by the Administration's NII task force in the fall of 1994.

This event signaled a new and stronger appreciation and utilization of the role of technology in Federal telecommuting. Prior to this activity, Federal telework had been, perhaps, overly cautious in stressing that telecommuting was not technology-dependent. In fact, as mentioned above, Federal use of the term 'Flexiplace' was based on a desire to demonstrate the independence of telework from technology.

GSA and DOT Team Up to Lead Federal Telework

As mentioned earlier, by 1994 it became very clear that given the telework assignments given to DOT and GSA, the two agencies should collaborate in leading the Federal telework movement. The implementation of this partnership was highlighted by a jointly produced revision of the Federal telecommuting manual (DOT, 1994). The efforts of these two agencies led to a new governmentwide telecommuting initiative, the National Telecommuting Initiative.

The National Telecommuting Initiative

In January 1996, in order to give Federal telework an apparently much-needed boost, the President's Management Council (PMC) implemented the National Telecommuting Initiative (NTI). The general mission of the NTI was to boost, primarily, the number of Federal teleworkers and, secondarily, the number of teleworkers in other sectors of the US workforce. Led by DOT and GSA in conjunction with an interagency taskforce, the NTI became the first governmentwide telework initiative to set numerical goals: 60,000 Federal teleworkers by October 1998 and 160,000 by the end of 2002.

One of the initial activities of the NTI was to conduct a survey of Federal agencies to determine the number of Federal teleworkers at the time (NTI, 1996). Agency response to the survey was hampered by the fact that few agencies had any established means of counting their teleworkers. The resulting uneven and possibly inaccurate response from the agencies indicated approximately 9,000 Federal teleworkers. In a subsequent audit of the aforementioned survey response, the US General Accounting Office (GAO) found numerous reporting errors. GAO concluded, however, that since understatements and overstatements were nearly equal, the reported total number of teleworkers could be assumed to be a reasonable, if shakey, estimate.

Over time, however, the NTI did not fare very well (See OPM Teleworker Count below). The expected boost in Federal teleworker numbers did not occur and by the end of 1998, GSA and DOT were considering ways to improve/reenergize the NTI. These planning efforts are still a work in progress.

In June 1996, following up on his 1994 Family Friendly Workplace memo to all Federal agencies, President Clinton directed agency heads to (1) review their personnel practices, (2) develop a plan of action to utilize the flexible policies already in place, (3) expand their ability to provide family friendly workplaces (including opportunities to telecommute), and (4) where feasible, to achieve the goal of 60,000 telecommmuters by 1998 as set by the President's Management Council. He further directed agencies to report their progress to the Vice President through the National Performance Review. "The National Performance Review, together with the Domestic Policy Council, the President's Management Council Working Group on Telecommuting, the Office of Personnel Management, and the General Services Administration will continue to work with the executive agencies as we move forward together to increase productivity through family friendly work environments."

RESEARCH FROM DOT

Also in 1996, Congress directed DOT to examine telecommuting issues such as the benefits and limitations of different approaches to implementation, keys to successful programs, and potential roles of Federal, state, and local governments in promoting telecommuting. In 1997, DOT published its research report, "Successful Telecommuting Programs in the Public and Private Sectors: A Report To Congress" (DOT, 1997). This assignment reflected the growing Federal interest in the development of all telework, not just Federal telework.

CONGRESSIONAL COALITION LETTER

In October 1996, still concerned about the lagging growth of Federal telework, a coalition of eight members of the House of Representatives wrote a letter to all agency heads extolling the value of telecommuting and encouraging exploration of telecommuting options available.

NATIONAL PERFORMANCE REVIEW AND THE NTI

In 1997, Vice President Gore communicated, to all Federal agencies, findings from a National Performance Review (NPR) analysis of agency reports on family friendly workplace progress. He noted "areas of achievement as well as areas which require a great deal more effort." One of the latter areas was telecommuting:

> ".... as many of you already understand, we must intensify our efforts to make telecommuting more readily available to our workers, not just in times of personal or medical emergency, but as an important management strategy. The accessibility of more than two dozen federal telecommuting centers, the advances in information technology, and the proven effectiveness of work-at-home arrangements, should give us the confidence that we can meet the challenge of 60,000 federal telecommuters by the end of fiscal year 1998....."

He urged agency heads to provide the strong leadership needed to create a family friendly workplace culture.

OPM PUBLICATIONS AND TELEWORKER COUNT

That same year, OPM issued a revised version of its 1995 publication, 'Balancing Work and Family Demands Through Telecommuting' (OPM, 1997), as well as a telework briefing tool called 'The Telework Briefing Kit' (OPM, 1997).

In early 1998, Reps Wolf and Hoyer requested OPM to conduct a study of Federal agency family friendly efforts and to include an update on telecommuting progress. In October 1998, OPM published its response to the Congressional request. A featured finding in the report was a case of good news/bad news. The good news was that the number of Federal teleworkers had grown to about 25,000. The bad news was that this was less than half of the PMC goal of 60,000 expected by that time. At approximately 1% of the Federal workforce, this finding was also significantly lower than the various estimates (ranging from 8% to 11%) for the percentage of teleworkers in the US workforce.

CONGRESSIONAL HEARINGS

Beginning in late 1999, the Congressional Workforce and Education Committee began a series of examinations and hearings into the reasons for the continuing slow growth of telework in the Federal government as well as in the U.S. workforce. This Congressional activity is underway as of this writing.

GSA/OPM TELEWORK POLICY REVIEW

In mid-1999, GSA and OPM began telework policy examinations in two directions. The first direction focused on existing workplace policy and its adequacy for supporting the Federal teleworkplace. For example, issues began to arise regarding the definition of an employee's official duty station and its relationship to regular and travel pay. It had become clear that numerous Federal workplace policies needed to be revised and/or clarified in view of the advance of telework (The importance of this activity was highlighted by a major public controversy over employer responsibility for home worksites - see OSHA below). The second direction focused on advancements in Federal telework such as working anytime/anywhere, alternative officing (hotelling, e.g.), and telework-assisted dependant care. It was clear that pilot tests and accompanying new policy were needed to implement these advanced aspects of telework. Currently, GSA and OPM are planning this activity.

THE OSHA CONTROVERSY AND INFORMATION AGE WORKPLACE POLICY

In November, 1999, the Occupational Safety and Health Administration (OSHA) of the US Department of Labor (DOL) issued an interpretation letter in response to an employer inquiry on employer responsibility for the safety and health conditions of teleworker home worksites. In essence, the letter implied that employers were responsible and liable for such conditions at teleworker home worksites. In January 2000, the OSHA letter was highlighted in a Washington Post article. This set off a firestorm of criticism and concern based on explicit aspects of the letter and implications drawn by the media, telework groups, Congress, and others. Rep. Wolf and others threatened Congressional action unless the letter was withdrawn. The DOL withdrew the letter and planned a detailed examination to be conducted in conjunction with relevant public and private organizations and experts. Prior to the examination, however, at a subsequent Congressional hearing, the DOL changed its official interpretation and stated that, except for dangerous manufacturing applications, employers would not be responsible/liable for the safety and health of home worksites.

Because of other problems as well as the need for further clarification of specific issues, Congress requested a continuation of plans for a collaborative detailed examination and report. The issue is still being deliberated as of this writing.

This was a significant event for at least two reasons. First, it highlighted the existing mismatch between information age workplace policy/practices and outdated industrial era policies, procedures, and management culture. This need for updating industrial era policy and procedure was pinpointed heavily in the Congressional hearings and attendant media coverage. Secondly, it signaled the advent of a major policy shift regarding employer responsibility and the safety and health of worksites in the information age.

CONCLUSION OF PART ONE

The above discussion covered, past to present, the general history of Federal telework. As you can see, at the time of this writing, there are new areas of telework action and energy that are beginning to unfold. In addition to general events, however, there were several streams of special applications of Federal telework that paralleled the general telework activity. These are discussed below.

PART TWO : SPECIAL APPLICATIONS OF FEDERAL TELEWORK

PEOPLE WITH DISABILITIES/WORKERS COMPENSATION

DOD PROGRAM FOR PEOPLE WITH DISABILITIES

In April of 1993, Judith Gilliom, a manager in the Department of Defense (DOD) Office of Civilian personnel, formally introduced telework as a DOD work option for people with disabilities. This Flexiplace project began with a one-year demonstration program. At the end of the demonstration period, the program transitioned into an on-going, supported work option. This was the first formal Federal effort to utilize the new Flexiplace initiative for people with disabilities:

> "The DOD program grew out of a larger effort to create new opportunities for persons with disabilities in the DOD civilian workforce. The goal was to create a diverse workforce in which at least 2% of all civilians employed would be employees with disabilities. Flexiplace was seen as a way of meeting that goal by offering an attractive work alternative to prospective employees. During the uncertain period of base closures, reductions in force, and changes in administration during the early 90's the DOD altered its goal from creating new opportunities to enhancing current positions" (Hesse, 1995, p. 419)

Findings from the demonstration program supported the conclusion that telework can be useful for persons with disabilities across a wide range of practice and should be a continuing work option. This DOD telework option for persons with disabilities is functioning actively today.

DOD CAP PROGRAM

Since its inception in 1990, DOD's Computer/Electronic Accommodations Program (CAP) has provided the equipment and assistive technology for people with disabilities to work at home or other alternate worksites (CAP, 1999). Working together, CAP and the DOD Flexiplace program for people with disabilities found that Flexiplace is an effective accommodation and recruitment tool for people with disabilities. CAP's target groups include:

- Recipients of workers' compensation payments;
- Persons who are being subjected to disability retirement;

- DOD employees with disabilities who could be more
productive if they were allowed to work part or all of the
week at home or in some other off-site location; and
- Persons with disabilities who have been unable to be
employed because their disabilities make it difficult for
them to function in a federal workplace on a regular basis.
Assistive devices supplied by CAP can:

- Allow injured employees to continue working in some
capacity;
- Help employees return to work after injury in a more
timely manner; and
- Help prevent further debilitation.

Today, CAP reports continuously increasing numbers of recipients
of its services.

EXECUTIVE MEMORANDUM ON EMPLOYING PEOPLE WITH SIGNIFICANT DISABILITIES UTILIZING ALTERNATE WORK SITES

In July 2000, President Clinton issued an executive memorandum
directing all Federal agencies to (1) identify positions that can
be relocated to alternate worksites and that can be filled by
qualified individuals, including those with significant
disabilities and (2) regarding the identified positions, develop
an action plan for encouraging the recruitment and employment of
qualified individuals with significant disabilities.

WORKERS COMPENSATION ACTIVITY

During the early 90's, agencies such as the Tennessee Valley
Authority, the Department of Labor, and DOD (as mentioned above)
began experimenting with the use of telework to (1) provide
opportunities for recipients of workers compensation and (2)
reduce the size and expense of the Workers' Compensation (WC)
Program.

Three major difficulties were uncovered:

- A risky situation for WC recipients who make the effort to
use telework to return to work (The risk is that if, for
some reason, the telework option does not work for the
recipient, the recipient may have a difficult time returning
to WC support.);
- A mistaken general belief by employers that WC recipients
are not interested in returning to work;

- An informal finding that some WC recipients would not be welcome back to their workplaces.

The latter two difficulties are program issues that could be overcome with a well-managed program initiative; the first difficulty (recipient risk), however, requires a legislative fix. Faced with such difficulties, efforts to develop a feasible and comprehensive telework option for Workers' Compensation faded out by the mid-90's. Various small initiatives continue to tackle this challenge. Currently, however, the absence of any Federal policy, legislation, and/or program established to bring the benefits of telework to Worker's Compensation continues to be a significant lost opportunity.

THE EMERGENCE OF FEDERAL TELECOMMUTING CENTERS (TELECENTERS)

The original Flexiplace guidelines called for pilot testing of telecenters as well as work-at-home programs. Telecenters are geographically convenient satellite offices shared by several agencies and/or other employers. 'Geographically convenient' refers to being established in locations close to the residences of potential Federal users. Telecenters serve the needs of those employees who want/need a reduced commute but who require the structure, social environment, technology, and/or other resources that are typically not available in a home setting.

Because work-at-home programs involved fewer resources and less complexity, the initial phase of Flexiplace focused on work-at-home programs as opposed to telecenters. In the summer of 1991, the Flexiplace project management team began planning/designing Federal telecenters. By that time, the project management team was an active participant in the Telecommuting Advisory Council (see ITAC, below). Inspired by Flexiplace updates at Council meetings, Marsha Fuller, a consultant from Hagerstown, Maryland, approached the project management team with the idea that Hagerstown would be a good pilot location for the telecenter initiative. Working with the project management team, Ms. Fuller was able to interest the Hagerstown mayor and business community in the idea. Thus, began the initial negotiations and concrete planning for the first Federal telecenter. Ironically, Hagerstown was not to be the first official Federal telecenter. Ms. Fuller mounted her own campaign on behalf of Federal telecenters. She was able to engineer helpful publicity as well as Congressional interest.

CONGRESSIONAL SUPPORT FOR FEDERAL TELECENTERS

In 1992, a variety of Washington DC area congressional representatives began work on establishing Federal telecenters. Tom McMillen (D, Md) began by drafting authorizing legislation that would place responsibility for development of Federal telecommuting in the Commerce Department (NTIA). In subsequent hearings held by McMillen, several testifying agencies (including Commerce) objected to the plan. This proposed legislation was soon dropped due partly to negative Federal reaction and, even moreso, to McMillen's re-election loss a few months later.

Meanwhile, on a separate Congressional front, Reps Hoyer (D, Md) and Wolf (R, Va) drafted appropriations language that would provide $5 million to fund three telecenters (one in Hoyer's district of southern Maryland, one in Wolf's district of northern Virginia, and one in McMillen's Maryland eastern shore district). In September 1992, this appropriation was approved and included in the Treasury, Postal, etc. Appropriations Bill (Public law 102-393;106 Stat. 1745). The purpose of the legislation was to test the effectiveness of telecenters in helping to alleviate area air quality and traffic congestion problems and in promoting a more family-friendly workplace.

As a result of further political activity, the preceding appropriation was amended (by Public Law 103-123; 107 Stat. 1241) in October, 1993. The amendment made the following changes:

- added an additional one million dollars to the appropriation,
- added Hagerstown, Md and Fredericksburg, Va to the list of telecenter pilot locations, and
- dropped the Maryland eastern shore district as a telecenter pilot location.

OFFICIAL OPENING OF FEDERAL TELECENTERS

Prior to the influx of Congressional funding, GSA and Hagerstown, assisted by private sector resources, established what can be called a preliminary telecenter located at the Hagerstown Junior College. While this was a worthwhile early effort, it was not an official Federal telecenter. Operation of official Federal telecenters began with the opening of the Winchester, Virginia telecenter. Between October 1993 and May 1994, GSA established four pilot telecenters in the greater Washington metropolitan area - two each in Maryland and Virginia. Initially, telecenters ranged from 10 to 30 workstations in size. The first four pilot telecenters offered a combined total of 80 workstations to 143 participants and achieved a workstation utilization rate of 55 percent by December 1994. Customer agencies paid a subsidized rate of $100 per workstation per month. Sites included:

- a 26-workstation facility in Winchester, Virginia in partnership with the U.S. Army Corps of Engineers Transatlantic Division and the Winchester-Frederick County Economic Development Commission (opened in October 1993 with 14 workstations);

- a 10-workstation facility at the Hagerstown Junior College in partnership with the City of Hagerstown and the U.S. Army Garrison at Fort Ritchie, Maryland (opened in October 1993);

- a 14-workstation facility in Charles County, Maryland in partnership with the Charles County Community College (opened in May 1994); and

- a 30-workstation facility in Spotsylvania County, Virginia (just south of Fredericksburg) in partnership with the Rappahannock Area Development Corporation (opened in May 1994).

By December 1994, 20 organizations in 10 Executive Branch Departments and Agencies were participating in the four centers. Agencies with the most significant participation included GSA, the Department of Defense (DOD), and DOT.

EMERGENCY RESPONSE: THE NORTHRIDGE EARTHQUAKE

In response to the Northridge (California) earthquake in 1994, GSA initiated the first use of telecenters as an emergency response measure. Only weeks after the January 17 earthquake, GSA established three emergency telecenters in the Los Angeles metropolitan area. These centers helped Federal workers avoid what for many had become a six-hour round-trip commute.

CUSTOMERS AS TELECOMMUTERS. Importantly, not only Federal employees benefitted from the markedly reduced commuting time afforded by the California emergency telecenters. Agency customers were also spared the long trip into downtown Los Angeles. For example, taxpayers in the Santa Clarita Valley could get help from IRS employees at the Valencia Telecommuting Center only five or ten minutes away. Similarly, veterans could substitute a tedious drive into west Los Angeles with a short, pleasant one to the same facility to receive guidance from a Department of Veterans Affairs (VA) benefits counselor.

Given management resistance to flexible workplace arrangements, even during an emergency, results were impressive through much of 1994. Despite little or no customer input on the location or size of the telecenters, utilization rates at two of the three telecenters were relatively high: the Valencia site (38 workstations) operated at 87 percent of capacity during the emergency while the 29-workstation Westlake site was at 62 percent utilization well into FY 1994. The Sherman Oaks site with 32 workstations was at 34 percent utilization at its peak. GSA made these centers available cost-free to interested agencies through the end of FY 1994 and experienced an overall utilization rate of 63 percent through the emergency period.

All told, ten Executive Branch Departments or Agencies participated in the Los Angeles area emergency telecenter effort including: GSA, IRS, VA, the Departments of Defense (DOD), Housing and Urban Development (HUD), Labor (DOL), Transportation (DOT), the Social Security Administration (SSA), the Office of Personnel Management (OPM), and the Corporation for National Service (CNS).

THE TELECENTER LESSON

The goal of the California Federal telecenters was twofold: to serve as an emergency response tool and to continue existing as an on-going telework option. In 1994, however, the emergency Federal telecenters experienced the following lesson which had been learned previously by non-Federal telecenters:

Telecenters emerged ahead of their time. In order to get started, most telecenters operated on a subsidy or emergency funding of some sort. This allowed them price their services at discount rates that were well below market rates and low enough to be a non-issue for employers. To succeed, however, these centers would need to be self-supporting. To achieve such independence, most telecenters eventually tried the obvious route of increasing their fees to market level rates. Raising fees to market levels, however, had the additional impact of putting telecenter fee levels on employer radar screens. Employers were faced with the prospect of paying the now-significant telecenter fees IN ADDITION TO the ongoing expenses for their teleworkers' main office space: thus, employers were paying double overhead for each teleworker using a telecenter. The bottom line result was that the raising of telecenter fees from discounted (subsidized) levels to market levels highlighted the double overhead problem and reduced the number of paying customers.

Another factor that reduced the number of paying customers was (and continues to be) ongoing management resistance to telework, in general, regardless of cost.

Two major culture changes would be required to make telecenters viable: (1) a changed management culture that would be more amenable to flexible workplaces, and (2) a changed organizational culture that would be receptive to alternative officing/space saving applications as part of more efficient facility management. For example, space vacated, partially or fully, by teleworkers would be released, consolidated, reconfigured, sub-leased etc. to reduce main office space costs; resulting cost savings would more than offset the typically lower costs for telecenter workstations. As of this writing, neither of the aforementioned culture changes has occurred in the majority of Federal workplaces. (For more detail on this discussion, see the section on alternative officing).

By December of 1994, due to the aforementioned issues, only one of the California emergency Federal telecenters (Valencia) continued to function. Given the mixed-use of this center, serving both telecommuters and customers, and its relatively high utilization rate, the Valencia site was able to continue to function with little or no subsidy.

OTHER CALIFORNIA PARTNERSHIPS

To build on this well-received start, GSA explored telecenter partnerships with state and local officials throughout California. These prospective partnerships were designed to make enterprising use of existing public assets (e.g., underutilized space, equipment, human resources), thus reducing the cost for telecenter participants and their employers. In these arrangements of low cost telecenter partnerships (which were designed for both public and private employer use), Federal agencies were tenants and paid a customer fee ranging from $100-$150 per workstation per month. By December 1994, for example, Federal employees had already begun telecommuting from four such sites in the Los Angeles area.

OTHER SPECIAL RESPONSE TELECENTERS: OKLAHOMA CITY AND ATLANTA

With the same expedience demonstrated in the aftermath of the Los Angeles earthquake, GSA established two emergency telecenters in the Oklahoma city area within weeks after the bombing of the Federal Building and four telecenters in Atlanta in response to traffic congestion needs associated with the 1996 Summer Olympics. As with the Los Angeles telecenters, these were not part of the aforementioned Congressional telecenter appropriation; these latter efforts were funded by special authority of the Federal Buildings Fund. While the Atlanta centers continue to operate, the Oklahoma centers have closed. The closure of the Oklahoma centers is not surprising since Oklahoma city was not on the list of areas having a high need for telecenter intervention for traffic congestion and/or air pollution.

THE NATIONAL GUARD BUREAU DISTANCE LEARNING/TELECENTER INITIATIVE

In 1995, the National Guard Bureau (NGB) was working on a major nationwide project to convert many of its armories into high-tech training centers capable of delivering distance-learning to guardspeople. Inspired by information on Federal telecenters, the NGB proposed and obtained a partnership with the Federal telecenter program. The partnership was based on the fact that the NGB expected to conduct its training activity in the training centers during non-business hours (evenings and weekends), leaving the centers free for telecenter use during normal business hours. In addition to improving the utilization and revenue for NGB armory/centers, this partnership provided a major increase in the number of Federal telecenter facilities and telecenter association with a well-funded national program. An additional benefit of the NGB partnership was that the NGB program brought a diversified revenue stream to the telecenter business: providing training and distance learning in addition to workstations. Telecenter managers had begun to realize that such diversification of their offerings could enhance their chances for success.

Thus, the NGB integrated telecenter workstations into its program offerings and, in conjunction with GSA, began establishing distance learning/telecenter facilities (primarily in Maryland). Due to a variety of inter-organizational difficulties, however, the NGB/GSA partnership eventually languished and currently exists minimally if at all. The NGB, however, has pushed ahead, on its own, with the integrated (distance learning + telecenter) model for its on-going initiative. Currently, the NGB has more than 180 distance learning facilities in operation.

MORE CONGRESSIONAL TELECENTER ACTIVITY

In 1996, in a continuing effort to jumpstart the generally underutilized Federal telecenters (Interagency Telecenter Program) in the Washington DC area, Congress passed a good news/ bad news bill. The good news was that
(1) GSA was authorized to 'establish, acquire space for, and equip' telecenters for use any public or private sector employee (Thus, not only was GSA formally authorized to get into the telecenter business, but GSA-sponsored telecenters would no longer be limited to Federal employee use.);
(2) telecenter user fees could be used to bolster telecenter program operating funds; and
(3) agency heads were requested to 'consider whether the need for ...facilities can be met using alternative workplace arrangements' such as telecommuting.
The bad news for the infant telecenter program was that for each individual telecenter, GSA would be required to charge user fees that would recover the costs of establishing and operating the center. This would result in significantly higher fees, possibly reducing utilization and killing the program.

By 1998, total Congressional funding for the Washington DC metropolitan area telecenters had reached $11 million dollars and the number of associated telecenters had grown to 16. In 1999, Reps Wolf and Hoyer authored additional telecommuting legislation. This language
(1) required Federal agencies to set aside an annual minimum of

$50,000 for telecenter user fees;
(2) appropriated an additional $2.1 million for telecenter development; and
(3) established a family friendly support office at OPM.

As of this writing, it has been less than a year since this legislation became law; its impact, thus far, has been minimal. The telecenters are quickly approaching a make or break point in their existence. As mentioned above, they have been gradually raising their user fees to attempt to recover costs and become self-sufficient. Interestingly enough, their customer base and overall utilization rates remain stable (possibly due to the $50,000 funding requirement mentioned above). It will be interesting to see if they can hold on until the culture of facility management becomes more amenable to their existence.

ENVIRONMENTAL IMPACT

CLIMATE CHANGE ACTION PLAN

In 1993, the White House published "The Climate Change Action Plan" focusing on environmental issues. Development of telework was one of the plan's action areas. The plan assigned EPA and DOT to take a series of actions designed to promote home-based and center-based telecommuting. The plan requested that:

> the U.S. Environmental Protection Agency (EPA), in consultation with DOT, issue guidance to states to take pro-telecommuting measures (e.g., reforming local zoning ordinances; providing employer trip reduction and tax incentives; and implementing telecommuting programs for state and local employees);
> DOT encourage states to use Federally provided transportation funds to initiate or expand telecommuting programs;
> DOT implement a Federal telecommuting pilot project with the goal of getting one to two percent of Federal employees to work at home at least one day a week; and
> DOT, in conjunction with other agencies, promote part-time, home-based telecommuting to reduce traffic congestion and promote energy conservation.

ENVIRONMENTAL IMPACT RESEARCH

In 1993, DOT became a major force in the development of Federal telecommuting when it published its now classic study on telework and transportation. Nicknamed the 'redbook' because of its bright red cover, 'Transportation Implications of Telecommuting' was the first comprehensive research-oriented treatment of this topic by a Federal entity. It is still widely used today.

Soon afterward, the Department of Energy published another transportation-related research report (DOE, 1994). This report provided detailed analysis of energy and emissions consequences of telework.

These latter reports finally gave Federal telework a sound empirical quantitative basis for its assertions of telework's environmental benefits. Both research efforts, however, faced a problem that continues today: the fact that teleworkers are not numerous enough to provide credible direct evidence on environmental impact. Consequently, both reports relied heavily on analysis via models and projected data. While both reports indicated future promise for telework impact on the environment (traffic congestion, air pollution, energy conservation), their estimates indicated modest impacts which served to tone down some of the claims being made by telework advocates.

TRAFFIC CONGESTION AND A PROPOSED EXECUTIVE ORDER

During the latter half of the 90's, most urban areas were being deluged by traffic congestion problems. Prominent among these was the Washington Metropolitan Area whose Board of Trade and council of local governments had repeatedly produced studies warning of the impending perils due to the increasing traffic congestion. In response to this, the Clinton Administration directed the DOT to take the lead on a Federal response. One of the resulting Federal responses was to set up an interagency effort to draft an executive order. The taskforce assigned to draft the order favored the inclusion of a strong statement on telecommuting that would require the Federal government to take on more responsibility by significantly reducing its share of the congestion.

Eight months after the original draft was submitted by DOT to OMB, however, it had not been signed into action and was considered dead in the water. This caused concern among some of the telework advocates in Congress and, in February 2000, Rep. Wolf introduced legislation to require the President to sign and implement the executive order. Shortly thereafter, OMB revised the draft executive order, deleting all mention of telework and focusing on transportation subsidies. President Clinton issued this version as executive order 13150 in the spring of 2000. Needless to say, this was a major source of consternation in the telework advocacy community.

CONGRESSIONAL ENVIRONMENTAL CREDIT PLAN

In the summer of 1999, motivated by mounting concerns over urban traffic congestion as well as the continuing slow development of telework, Rep. Wolf, now chairman of the House Appropriations Subcommittee on Transportation, introduced a bill to pilot test financial incentives to businesses that let employees work from home on various days. Rep. Wolf's pilot program, to be conducted in five metropolitan areas, would give voluntarily participating firms pollution credits that they would be free to sell in deals with other businesses and nonprofit groups, Federal and state governments and schools and universities. The bill was enacted into law and a task force that includes DOT, EPA, and DOE was established to design and implement the program. The design effort is currently underway.

ALTERNATIVE OFFICING

In the mid 1990's, a new driver for Federal telework began to surface. This driver is reduced facility costs. It was noted that with sufficient utilization of telework, an agency could reconfigure its main worksite to take advantage of the fact that at least part of the time, there could be a significant amount of work space, vacated by teleworkers, that is not in use. The resulting reconfiguration based on options such as hotelling, mini-workstations, desk sharing, team space, etc. could enable employers to achieve significant reductions in operating costs through reductions in main worksite space, through leasing or sub-leasing of main worksite space, and/or through consolidations of main worksite space.

This 'alternative officing' is a by-product of the telework movement. Because it requires a new management view toward the possession and handling of office real estate, it is a culture-change movement in itself.

THE FEDERAL RAILROAD ADMINISTRATION ALTERNATIVE OFFICING ACTIVITY

(From July 28, 1999, FEDERAL RAILROAD ADMINISTRATION'S REPORT ON TELECOMMUTING)

In 1995, the Federal Railroad Administration (FRA) implemented a telecommuting plus alternative officing program in 22 Railroad Safety Inspector field offices around the country. Safety Inspectors who volunteered for the program telecommuted full-time from their homes and their traditional office space was eliminated. By January 1997, the FRA had closed seven field offices, reduced space in two others, and saved approximately $80,000. In FY 1997, the FRA closed 5 more field offices and reduced space in 3 offices resulting in an annual savings of $84,644. In FY 1998, FRA closed 6 field offices and reduced space in 4 offices, resulting in a cost savings of $87,285. As of this writing, no new FRA field offices have been established.

In this case, telecommuting was not considered a condition of employment and participating employees could elect to terminate their arrangements with 3 months advance notice. FRA would then be required to find and provide traditional workspace for the telework-terminating inspector(s). As of this writing, only one telecommuting inspector has requested termination of his telecommuting arrangement. Approximately 65% (185 employees) of the FRA's inspector workforce telecommutes on a permanent basis.

Current FRA telecommuting goals continue to be focused on reducing facility costs, improving employees' well-being through maximization of participation and improving operational efficiency.

ALTERNATIVE OFFICING AT THE DEPARTMENT OF EDUCATION AND OTHER AGENCIES

In 1996, the Department of Education used an alternative officing solution to deal with budgetary problems. Using a combination of hotelling and home workstations, Education was able to reduce facility costs in regional field office locations. These savings enabled Education to save 24 jobs that otherwise would have been lost.

Other agencies that have reported alternative officing activity are the Consumer Product Safety Commission and the Defense Contract Audit Agency.

THE INTERNATIONAL TELEWORK ASSOCIATION (ITAC)

In the early 90's, at the very beginning of the PCMI Flexiplace initiative, Federal planners realized that telework activity spanned far beyond the Federal sector and that information, support, technical assistance, and numerous other benefits could be obtained by joining a small but growing advocacy group which at that time was called the Telecommuting Advisory Council (now called the International Telework Association and Council). OPM and GSA both participated actively in ITAC; GSA is still heavily involved in ITAC. Over the years, ITAC and Federal agencies partnered on numerous mutually beneficial activities in support of the telework movement. One of the primary partnership activities, which began in 1995, was 'Telecommute America!' which is discussed below.

TELECOMMUTE AMERICA! (NOW CALLED TELEWORK AMERICA!)

In 1994, after conducting a successful event which set aside a special day for company-wide telecommuting and telecommuting focused activity, AT&T contacted EPA, GSA, and the Association for Commuter Transportation (ACT). AT&T's purpose was to propose a similar activity on a national scale. Out of these discussions emerged plans for Telecommute America! (now called Telework America!). Telework America! (TWAM) is a public/private partnership designed to promote and support the growth of telecommuting in the US. TWAM's initial founding sponsors included AT&T, EPA, GSA, ACT, ITAC, and the US Department of Commerce. Using major funding from AT&T and EPA, TWAM was implemented as a week-long, nationwide slate of telework events in 1995. The Federal government has used TWAM as a forum to focus attention on its telework movement. Today, TWAM is still a public/private partnership but is now a year-round, international activity run by ITAC.

A SPECIAL PARTNER: WMCOG

The coincidence of the following factors created an on-going partnership between the Federal telework program and the Washington Metropolitan Council of Governments (WMCOG):

- the growing traffic congestion problem in the DC metropolitan area (now rated as the second worst congestion in the nation),
- the fact that the primary leaders of Federal telework are located in the DC area, and
- the fact that the primary location for Federal telecenters is the DC metro area.

Though based and focused in the DC area, COG became a major champion and supporter for Federal telework and telecenters. This support includes funding and other resources as well as services.

TODAY

As mentioned in the beginning of this discussion, the Federal telework program is still evolving. Reading through this discussion, one can see that, in fact, there is a lot of telework activity unfolding at this time. Federal telework is not yet a mainstream arrangement and, certainly, there are some serious challenges ahead. All in all, however, things look promising for telework as well as much needed true progress into the information age.

Reference List

Carlisle, N. (1991). _Report On State Agency Responses To Work-at-Home in Region 9_. San Francisco, California: EPA Office of Planning and Management.

Cohen, D. (1999). _The DOD Computer/Electronic Accommodations Program (CAP)_. E-mail Message. US Department of Defense. Washington DC

Cowley, T.N., & Joice, W.H. (1989) _Informal Work-at-home Arrangements in the Federal Government_. US General Services Administration. Washington DC. Unpublished report

DOT. (1993). _Transportation Implications of Telecommuting_. Washington DC: US Department of Transportation. U.S. G.P.O.: 1993-343-120:85869

DOT. (1997). _Successful Telecommuting Programs in the Public and Private Sectors: A Report to Congress_. Washington DC: US Department of Transportation.

Energy. (1994). _Energy, Emissions, and Social Consequences of Telecommuting_. Washington DC: US Department of Energy: Office of Policy, Planning, and Program Evaluation. DOE/PO-0026

FRA. (1999). _Federal Railroad Administration Report on Telecommuting_. Washington DC: Federal Railroad Administration, US Department of Transportation.

GAO. (1992). _The Changing Workforce: Comparison of Federal and Nonfederal Work/Family Programs and Approaches_. Washington DC: US General Accounting Office. GAO/GGD-92-84

Hesse, B.W. (1995). Curb Cuts in the Virtual Community: Telework and Persons with Disabilities. In _Proceedings of the 28th Annual Hawaii International Conference on System Sciences:_ Hawaii

Joice, W.H. (1989) _Home-Based Employment: A Solution to Federal Government Recruiting Problems_. US Office of Personnel Management. Washington DC. Unpublished Report

Joice, W.H. (1991). Home Based Employment: A Consideration for Public Personnel Management. _Public Personnel Management, 20_(1), 49-60.

Joice, W.H. (1993). _The Federal Flexible Workplace Pilot Project Work-at-Home Component_. Washington DC: US Office of Personnel Management. PRD 92-15

Joice, W.H. (1994). _Implementing Telecommuting_. Washington DC: US Department of Transportation.

Landon, L.W. (1991). We Didn't Fall Through the Cracks. _HR Magazine,_ 48-50.

Master, W., & Joice, W.H. (1994). Promoting Telecommuting: An Application of the NII. Germantown, Maryland: National Institute of Standards and Technology, US Department of Commerce. Special Publication 868,73-87.

National Analysts. (1991). Qualitative Evaluation of EPA Region 9's Work-At-Home Experience. Booz Allen & Hamilton.

Nilles, J. (1999). Perspectives on the History of Federal Telework. E-mail Message. JALA International. Los Angeles, California

NIST. (1994). The Information Infrastructure: Reaching Society's Goals. Germantown, Maryland: National Institute of Standards and Technology, US Department of Commerce. Special Publication 868

NPR. (1993). Creating a Government That Works Better & Costs Less: Report of the National Performance Review. Washington DC: National Performance Review.

NTI. (1996) National Telecommuting Initiative Survey of Federal Agencies. US General Services Administration. Washington DC. Unpublished Report

OMB. (1989). Management for Fiscal Year 1990. Washington DC: US Office of Management and Budget. 2-32-2-32.

OPM. (1991). Federal Flexible Workplace (Flexiplace) Project. Washington DC: US Office of Personnel Management. FPM Letter 368-1

OPM. (1997). Telework Briefing Kit. Washington DC: US Office of Personnel Management.

OPM. (1998). A Review of Family-Friendly Workplace Arrangements. Washington DC: US Office of Personnel Management.

PCMI. (1990). Guidelines for Pilot Flexible Workplace Arrangements. Washington, DC: President's Council on Management Improvement. GSA Printed Document

Schiff, F.W. (1979). Working At Home Can Save Gasoline. The Washington Post, September 2, 1979, Washington DC: The Washington Post Company

Schiff, F.W. (1993) Comments On the Origins of Flexiplace. MATAC. Washington DC. Unpublished Presentation to the Mid-Alantic Telecommuting Advisory Council

The Hudson Institute. (1987). Workforce 2000. Washington DC: US Department of Labor.

The Hudson Institute. (1988). Civil Service 2000. Washington, DC: US Office of Personnel Management. CE-56

Wheeler, T. (1990). White House Keeps Tab on Federal Flexiplace. Flexiplace Focus, April 1990, p2 Washington DC: US Office of Personnel Management

Wheeler, T. (1992). Congress Agrees on Proposal for Telecommuting Study.
 <u>Flexiplace Focus,</u> February 1992, p1-2, Washington DC: US Office of
 Personnel Management